MEDICARE
MADE 123 EASY

Includes 2016 Health Changes

Just the facts,
No gimmicks,
No sales pitches,
Just what you
need to know

DAVID & IAN SCHAEFFER

Medicare Made 123 Easy

Copyright © 2016 by David P. Schaeffer and Ian M. Schaeffer
Illustrations of Easy Eddie Copyright © 2016 by Ian M. Schaeffer
All Rights Reserved.

Published by LuLu

To order additional copies of this title, contact your local bookstore or call 877-220-1089.

The author may be contacted at the following address:
American Retirement Advisors
4909 E. Armor St.
Cave Creek, AZ 85331
Phone: 877-220-1089
Email: david@ARA123.com
Web sites: www.AmericanRetire.com

Cover Graphic, Cover Design and Page Design by Ian M. Schaeffer
Original edit by Steven Jay Thor

Printed in the USA by LuLu
Initial Printing, August 2012
Second Edition, January 2013
Third Edition, January 2014
Fourth Edition, January 2015
Fifth Edition, January 2016

Schaeffer, David P. & Schaeffer, Ian M.
Medicare Made 123 Easy. Just the facts, No gimmicks, No sales pitches, Just what you need to know / David and Ian Schaeffer

ISBN   978-1-300-07296-6

   1. Selecting a Medicare Plan   2. Medicare Supplements
             3. Medicare Advantage Plans

FOREWARD

"Just as I told you in 2011, when you wrote the first copy, I remain very "high" on this book. Not only does it explain Medicare and Medicare Supplement Insurance well, it does it in language so simple…"

Kevin Michael Lynch
MBA, CFP®, CLU®, ChFC®, RHU, REBC, CASL®, CAP®, LUTCF, FSS

Assistant Professor of Insurance
The Charles Zimmerman Chair of Life Insurance Education

Table of Contents

Appendices

Introduction

Sally: "Hey honey. Look, we got another card, this time from
Super Duper Insurance Company."

John: "I know, I know…It's the hundredth one this month!"

Sally: "Well, shouldn't we do something about it?"

John: "I would but, there is so much information, I don't even know where to begin, with: enrollment periods, health restrictions, provider restrictions, Medicare Part A, Medicare Part D, Medicare Advantage, Medigap…It's just TOO much!"

Sound like a familiar story? Maybe that's why you picked up this book? Or, maybe you're just curious about how the whole process works. Whatever the reason, I'm glad you did! We will make this whole process easier for you.

Now, I've read all the books with titles that say: "Look here, we can help!" or, "Hey. Here's all the information you'll ever need." Every time I read these headlines I get a wrenching tingle at the bottom of my stomach; because, you know, it flat out hurts to be fooled.

What I found, was that there is always a bias and always something in the story to make you want to purchase one thing or another.

The simple reality is that EVERY SITUATION IS UNIQUE and plans…well, they change. There is just no way to peddle one product and label it as the "Best" for everyone. I see why it happens though. With so many people out there trying to get at your money, they have to do something to be noticed. I grew tired of hearing clients coming to me so misinformed and so distraught about the Medicare process that I decided to do something more to help.

I thought about healthcare, money, estates, then their legacy and a plethora of other concerns; and I thought about how I could make all of this better…the word that kept coming to mind…well, was the word "EASY". Everybody loves easy, from choosing which frozen luncheon entrée to pop in the microwave to retiring. It shouldn't be any different. 1-2-3 Easy… That was it! It became our goal. With the help of my little friend, Easy Eddie, who you will meet later, we are going to illustrate this process question-by-question and step-by-step.

Let's start talking about Medicare. A major concern that often comes to my mind is: "What is it?" And "What is it going to cover?" Another concern may be, "Am I going to have to buy more than what the government provides for me? When can I enroll? When does it go into effect? Do I need an insurance agent? If so, how do I know that they have my best interest in mind?"

There should be a guide to walk you through it step-by-step, don't you think? 1-2-3 Easy. That's the name of my game, and the mantra to my practice.

This book will provide you the tools you will need to make the very best choices you possibly can when it comes to making decisions for each of the questions listed on the previous page and more. What follows are some of the professional 'legalese' terms, broken down into plain English, common misinformation explained, and a step by step guide to the Medicare process. From applying for Social Security and Original Medicare, to Medicare Advantage plans.

I want to make sure that by the end of this book you have, at the very least, a much clearer understanding of what 1-2-3 Easy feels like, and **how to ask the right questions** as you move forward with your Medicare decisions.

Allow me to introduce **Easy Eddie**. He is here to help walk us through this maze by providing some handy tips as we go.

Hi, I'm Eddie!

The best way I see to do this is to go through the process as if I, or my mother, were gearing up to deal with turning 65 and applying for Medicare.

Now, my situation may not be exactly the same as yours, but I will do my best to explain each option and provide extra resources for you to explore more of what is best for your particular case. In addition to all the needed information, I will try and break it up a bit with some questions and charts to make sure that the information sinks in just a little easier, and **Easy Eddie** will be there with us <u>every step of the way</u> helping us to better understand each part of the process.

If you are ready, let's dive in!

$$ Medicare $$

Advantage

Savings

Medigap

Long Term Care

Investments

Retirement

Chapter One:
Getting Started

"It is my passion to turn the complex into 123 Easy."

-David P. Schaeffer

So where do we start?

Let's go ahead and say the biggest concern at the moment is defining Medicare. What is 'It'? What am I even supposed to do? When can I do something about it?

In a nutshell, Medicare is health insurance standardized by the federal government for people age 65 or older. But, inside of Medicare there are more intricacies that will be brought to light in the next few pages.

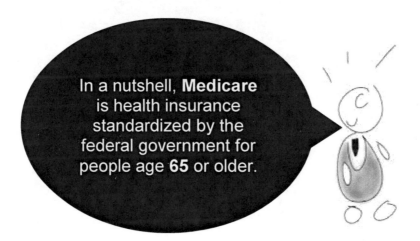

Let's start with the **Basic Medicare**; which consists of Parts A and B, with the addition of an *optional* Part D. This is also known as **Original Medicare**.

Part A

Part A is essentially hospital insurance. After a per-occurrence deductible ($1,288 in 2016) is met. Part A helps to cover 80% of inpatient care as well as skilled nursing facilities, hospice, and home health care services. A complete list can be found in Appendix A at the end of this book.

If you or spouse of 10 years or more have been working for 40 quarters (10 years of full time work) in the United States, you have already been paying into Medicare. Therefore, there is usually no charge for Medicare Part A.

Still Working?

If you are turning 65, but currently working and want to wait to take your Social Security benefits, then you would call Social Security directly at **1-800-772-1213** to enroll in Medicare Part A. If you are already receiving Social Security then you will automatically be enrolled in Medicare Parts A and B, and should receive your Medicare card in the mail 100 days prior to your 65th birthday. The premium for Part B will be automatically taken out of your Social Security benefit check each month. Medicare premiums are due the month before your Medicare becomes effective.

Not Working?

If you are turning 65 and are not working, you have a couple of choices. If you are not taking Social Security yet, refer to the paragraph on the previous page labeled "Still Working" and follow the process as directed. However, if you are already receiving Social Security checks in the mail, you will automatically be enrolled in Medicare Parts A and B. You will receive your Medicare card in the mail, with your Part B premium (which covers 80% of doctor's charges) automatically taken out of your Social Security check each month. This deduction will be $104.90 per month for those already on Medicare and collecting Social Security or $121.80 for those not yet on Medicare (2016) or more depending upon your income. See information about Part B further on in this section.

Covered by your current employer?

If you are turning 65 and are covered under your current employer's group health plan, call the benefits department to check and see if they require you to have Parts A and B of Medicare. If not, you are in a DO NOTHING situation. 90 days prior to leaving your group health plan, it will be time to begin the Medicare enrollment process. When you are no longer covered under your employer group health plan, you are starting with a clean slate and an open enrollment period that begins at that point because you were still working at age 65 and covered by your employer healthcare at the time of your initial enrollment period. No penalties will apply. You may choose to enroll in a plan of your choice up to 30 days prior to the termination of your employer group coverage.

Cost vs. Coverage

Now, it is quite possible to be in the situation where you are not sure whether you want to switch from your current coverage (employee or retiree group) to a Medicare Advantage or Medigap plan. This will take some thought and analysis. It will come down to a couple of factors: the cost of the coverage, your satisfaction with your current plan, and undoubtedly what medical necessities individual plans cover. Keep these things in mind as you continue. It will help with the selection process.

Part B

Part B is simply medical insurance. It provides assistance with the cost of doctor visits and other services that do not involve a hospital stay. There is a monthly premium (cost of insurance) for Part B. This premium is standardized at $104.90 as of 2016 for those already collecting Social Security and on Medicare but it will be $121.80 for those not yet on Medicare. (It can be higher depending on income. See an income chart in Appendix C).

What is covered?

Medical necessities such as doctor visits, ambulatory surgery services, some preventative care like immunizations, blood work, x-rays, and some diagnostic screenings. (A complete list can be found in Appendix B).

What it doesn't it cover?

It does not cover any care outside of the United States. It does not cover the cost of help with daily activities (such as bathing, eating, or getting dressed), nor any care of eyes, teeth, or hearing.

How does it work then?

Part B generally covers 80% of the cost of services after an annual deductible ($166 in 2016). For example, I go to a doctor and as a result, I need an MRI which may cost $1000. Let's do some math. The Medicare Part B deductible in 2016 is $166. After that, Part B covers 80% of the medical expense, in this case the $1000 MRI. Here it is broken down.

1) $1000 (MRI) - $166 (deductible)
= **$834 (Balance)**

2) 20% of $834 (NOT covered by Part B)
= **$166.80**

3) $166.80 + $166 (deductible)
= **$332.80**

Bottom line: out of pocket I would pay **$332.80**. We will cover how to fill this gap of $332.80 in coverage a little later.

Part D

(Optional... *sort of*)

Part D is prescription drug coverage. It helps to cover the cost of prescription drugs. This part can get a bit tricky, so bear with me for a minute. In exchange for an average premium of $32.50 a month you receive an initial coverage of $3,310. Some plans have an annual deductible of up to $360, while others do not have any deductible at all. After the initial coverage of $3,310, there is a coverage gap until you and the Part D provider have spent $4,850. At that point, catastrophic coverage comes in and you pay $2.95 to $7.40 per prescription. It's confusing I know, but essentially what you need to know is that in counties across the country there are as many as 30 different drug plans to choose from. These can be found on Medicare's website at www.Medicare.gov.

Appendix F offers a click-by-click example of how to go through this process. The website is useful, but tricky to navigate. It is important that you pay close attention to the options being listed. We will simplify and help you to customize a plan that is best for your specific needs. Just a warning: this drug plan selection process on Medicare's website is not easy no matter how detailed a guide I provide in this book. If you would rather talk to Medicare representatives directly you can call 1-800-MEDICARE (1-800-633-4227). I would highly recommend finding an insurance agent who is experienced in Medicare that you trust. Chapter Six shares some questions for you to ask your insurance agent to ensure that they truly have your best interest in mind.

What are my other options?

Everything we discuss from this point forward is based on the assumption that you will be enrolled in Parts A and B of Medicare. Basic Medicare has gaps. The rest of the book will be discussing how to fill them.

Review

Let's just review for a second. We know now that **Original Medicare** includes Parts A and B, with the suggested addition of a Part D for prescription drugs. We know that **Part A** only helps to cover things associated with hospital stays. **Part B** only covers 80% of medical necessities after an annual deductible. The suggested **Part D** is your prescription drug coverage.

Chapter Two:
Closing the Gap

"Medicare Supplements offer choices. Medicare Advantage plans help your monthly budget."

-David P. Schaeffer

What are my choices?

There are two main choices if you do not have group benefits as an employee or retiree: 1) You can choose to supplement your Medicare benefits with a federally standardized Medicare Supplement also known as a Medigap Plan, or 2) You can choose to transfer (actually replace) your Medicare benefits to a Medicare Advantage plan sometimes referred to as Part C of Medicare.

1) Supplementing my benefits

With this option, you will supplement your Medicare benefits with a Medigap Plan. This is one of a series of federally standardized plans (A-N) that are issued through a third party insurance company (these are those brochures from insurance companies you are probably being bombarded with in the mail.) A federal grid of these plans is provided in the Medicare packet that you have, or can receive in the mail from the government. You can look in Appendix H where we provided one for you as well.

Every single one of these plans, no matter which insurance company you choose, are **EXACTLY THE SAME!** A Medigap Plan F from Company XYZ is exactly the same as a Medigap Plan F from Company ABC. The only thing that will differ is the premium you pay for the plan.

A Medigap Plan F from Company XYZ is **EXACTLY THE SAME** as a Medigap Plan F from Company ABC. The only thing that will differ is the premium you pay for the plan.

Medigap plans cover you anywhere in the United States.
This means that you can purchase a Medicare Supplement (Medigap) and receive primary care, urgent care, or emergency care anywhere in the United States. Premiums for these plans will vary by insurance carriers, but as we already stated, coverage is EXACTLY THE SAME because it is federally standardized, and Medicare actually processes your claims.

A grid of each one of the plans A-N can be found on Medicare's website www.Medicare.gov.

The **Medigap Plan F** serves to fill all the "gaps" in coverage of Original Medicare. That means the 20% you would have had to pay, including the co-pays and deductibles for doctor visits, hospital stays, and labs would now be taken care of. Simply put, you pay $0 out of pocket for your medical needs. You will only pay your monthly premium for your Medicare Part B and your Medigap Plan.

Remember the MRI?

1) $1000 (MRI) - $166 (deductible)
= $834 (Balance)

2) 20% of $834 (NOT covered by Part B)
= $166.80

3) $166.80 + $166 (deductible)
= $332.80

4) MRI with Medigap Plan F
= $0

2) Transferring (replacing) My Benefits

With this option we do just that. Our Medicare Benefits are transferred to a third party insurance company. This is called **Medicare Advantage** where Medicare will simply pay the provider a flat rate, and the insurance company would then pay for the cost of your care.

Here is an example. "**SuperCare**" is a Medicare Advantage plan. When you choose to replace your Medicare benefits with *SuperCare*, this company is now responsible for covering your medical needs, instead of Medicare itself. Medicare pays *SuperCare* a flat rate, which then pays the majority of your medical expenses. You simply pay the co-pays for each service provided.

These plans can range in premiums from $0 to $180 and are generally in the form of Health Maintenance Organizations (HMO's), Preferred Provider Organizations (PPO's) and Private Fee-For-Services Plans (PFFS's).

With each one of these, there are typically co-pays. In the worst case scenario, you can expect to pay a maximum of $6,700 out of pocket per year, but for many Medicare Advantage plans this cap is much less. Additionally, unlike Medigap plans, the Medicare Part D prescription drug coverage is generally included.

The reason many people choose a Medicare Advantage plan is because of monthly cost. Generally, Medicare Advantage plans are less expensive than Medigap plans and if your doctors are in the network, then this choice is logical. Also, if you are a person who does not need to see a doctor very often, a Medicare Advantage plan might make more sense, since the monthly premiums will be much less than a Medigap plan.

Review

We now know a little bit about each of our options. We can supplement our basic Medicare with a Medigap plan, or we can transfer our Medicare benefits to a third party and let the Medicare Advantage plan take care of our medical needs.

Chapter Three:
Let's Compare

"Access to quality medical care has less to do with the brands we know, than the networks they are contracted to represent."

-David P. Schaeffer

Below, these two programs are compared side-by-side. On the left, **Easy Eddie** shows you an example using the **Medigap Plan F**, which in most instances provides the most comprehensive coverage and a way to eliminate any of those surprise medical costs. On the right, Eddie is presenting the range of costs possible with a **Medicare Advantage Plan**.

As of now, in most cases, there is no cost for Medicare Part A. However, in 2016 for Part B there is a flat rate of $121.80 a month (for those not currently on Medicare and collecting Social Security), but that varies by income level (Appendix C). Now, the Medigap monthly premiums may range from $121 to $362 a month at age 65, prescription drug plans range from as little as $11.40 a month to $174.70 for Enhanced Drug Plans.*

Medigap Plan F		Medicare Advantage Plan	
Medicare Part A	$ 0.00*	Medicare Part A	$ 0.00*
Medicare Part B	$ 121.80**	Medicare Part B	$ 121.80**
Medigap Premium	($121-$362) $ 150	Medicare Advantage Premium	($0-$188) $0
Medicare Part D	$ 33	Medicare Part D (usually included)	$ 0
	$ 304.80 per month		**$ 121.80 per month**
*See Chapter One **Appendix C All values are averages based on plans as of January 2016 (premiums vary by zip code)		*See Chapter One **Appendix C All values are averages based on plans as of January 2016 (premiums vary by zip code)	

*The Henry J Kaiser Family Foundation October 13, 2015

What does "Enhanced Drug Plan" mean?

Here is an example...

On one side of the room, let's put Fred. Fred is a healthy guy who has been fortunate enough to not be taking any pills, and doesn't plan on ever taking any prescription medication. So, he may want to go with an $11.40 plan, because he doesn't need a lot of coverage.

Now let's meet Mike and stand him on the other side of the room. Mike hasn't been as fortunate as Fred. Mike is taking a total of 15 pills a day to keep healthy. As of now, his prescriptions are costing him $3,000 a month! He could use some help paying for all that or he might go broke well before he should! So, he would likely be looking at $175 a month plan with a $100 copay that includes his non-generic specialty drugs at a reasonable cost. Because hey, $175 looks a whole lot better than $3,000 to me. In any case, please refer to Appendix F for a click-by-click guide using Medicare's website to find out which plan is best for you based on the prescription medications you are currently taking.

On the **Medicare Advantage** side, we see that Medicare Parts A and B are identical across the board. It is when we get to premiums that things change. As I pointed out earlier, premiums range from $0 a month to costing you $188; but, prescription drug plans are typically included. I just wanted to reiterate this as you begin your search for what is right for your needs. If you choose to go with Basic Medicare (Parts A, B, & D) plus a Medigap plan, it DOES NOT matter which insurance carrier you select.

Medicare Supplements (Medigap) are offered by insurance carriers under strict guidelines standardized by the federal government, which assures their congruity or 'sameness'. For example, Medicare Supplement Plan F from one company is 100% exactly the same as a Plan F offered by any other carrier.

There are currently 10 federally standardized Medigap plans offered in 47 States (exception states: Minnesota, Wisconsin and Massachusetts). These are Plans A-N. The most comprehensive is Plan F, which I discussed earlier (see Appendix H).

What if I decide to select a Medicare Advantage Plan?
Well, Medicare Advantage Plans have standardized benefits, but the co-pays and networks differ by plan. Selecting a Medicare Advantage Plan has more to do with the network of doctors and hospitals than with the plan.

So how do I go about choosing one?

I have provided a worksheet in Appendix G that will combine all of this information, allowing you to go through this process on your own. The remainder of this chapter will break down our Medicare Advantage Plan Selection Process into even further detail.

Our Medicare Advantage Plan Selection Process.

1. **Identify PHYSICIANS important to your care.**
2. **Identify HOSPITALS important to your care.**
3. **Identify the PRESCRIPTIONS important to your care.**
4. **Search each Provider Directory.**
5. **Find the Plan that has the most matches!**
6. **Compare Benefits of all plans meeting your needs!**

Step 1: *Identify Physicians Important to your Care*

If you are currently happy with your doctor, (most people are) see if they are in your desired network. If he or she is not covered in the Medicare Advantage Network, a Medigap plan may be a better option for you.

Step 2: *Identify Hospitals Important to your Care*

My dad (for real) is one of those guys who goes to the hospital for everything! Sometimes it may be necessary, other times we aren't sure if he is just going to talk to the staff; but to him, the hospital is important. Thus, the plan he chose reflected such a concern. If you like a place, there should be no reason you should have to leave it simply based on the coverage you select. Again, I want to reiterate, an agent or broker will be more than happy to help you determine which option is best for your particular needs.

Step 3: *Identify Prescriptions Important to your Care*

This is where Eddie gets to talk to you about picking a drug plan. The steps are very similar between choosing a Part D and a Medicare Advantage plan for drugs. Appendix G has a worksheet that can help you with both.

Step 4: *Search Each Plan's Provider Directory*

Search each plan's network **directly**. Do not ask the doctor's office! I'm not saying that it's bad to call your doctors; but the people behind the desk answering the phone are not legally held accountable for providing you with accurate information. Most of the time it is because they are not asked the right questions. If you call and ask, "Do you take Medicare?" "No". That's false! If you call the doctor and ask do you take Blue Cross?" The answer will most likely be "Yes." Great, Blue Cross offers Group Health, Government Group Health, HMO's, PPO's, Medicare Advantage, Medicare Supplements (Plans A-N), and more. They have no idea which network you are asking about.

Simply put, because the person on the other end of line does not know which plan you have, they cannot possibly give you an accurate answer, unless he or she knows your plan and goes to the individual plan's network directory themselves. To avoid all the hassles, go straight to the plan's network directory **first**! Then, verify with the **billing department** at the doctor's office.

Step 5: *Choose the Plan with the Most Matches*
I hope you find that this is pretty self-explanatory. Check www.ismydocinthenetwork.com for links to National Provider Directories, or you can check each provider's website directly.

Step 6: *Compare Benefits of all the Plans Meeting Your Needs*
This step is tricky only because there may be several plans that provide all of the benefits that you are looking for on the

surface. However, just like with groups, such as AARP, there are additional benefits that may come with being a part of a larger organization. These additional benefits are sometimes worth looking into.

Appendix G provides a selection tool to help you when choosing plans, whether this means **Medicare Advantage, Medigap, Prescription Drug Plans**, or all of the above.

Chapter Four:
Prescription Drug Plan Selection

"Selecting a Medicare Part D prescription drug plan is all about matching the formulary, pharmacy and co-pays to your current need. It has little to do with the brand or company that offers the plan."

-David P. Schaeffer

What is the selection process?

The process of selecting the most appropriate Medicare Part D plan for your current needs is actually easier than explaining the rules surrounding a Medicare Part D prescription drug plan. So, let's begin by separating Medicare Part D into four sections.

Section 1: *The Deductible*

Under Medicare's standard model, a Part D prescription drug plan may include a deductible of up to $360 for 2016. If the plan indeed does have a deductible, you must pay it completely before you receive any benefits.

Section 2: *The Initial Coverage Limit*

This is $3,310 for 2016. Essentially, this is the amount of coverage you initially receive in exchange for your premium. In English, this is the initial pool of benefit money in your plan. To reach this initial coverage amount, subtract the plan's negotiated retail price of the prescriptions from the pool of benefit money until the benefit money pool is empty. Once you've used the initial coverage limit, we move to the coverage gap (the donut hole).

Section 3: *The Coverage Gap*

This part gets a bit sticky, so hang in there. We need to get from $3,310 retail cost spent on your behalf to $4,850. That is the coverage gap. In the coverage gap, you pay 45% of the retail cost of a non-generic prescription. The prescription drug plan pays 5% and the manufacturer of the drug pays 50%. This takes place until all parties have spent a total of $4,850 on prescriptions drugs.

You may have to read though this section a couple of times to understand it.

Section 4: *Catastrophic Coverage*

Once you reach the catastrophic coverage section you pay the greater of 5% or $2.95 for generic drugs. For brand named drugs you pay the greater of 5% or $7.40.

On the next page is a simplified example of the math that goes with a $6,000 annual retail prescription drug cost and 33% co-pay tier drug.

2016 Medicare Prescription Drug Co-Pay Example
Example of a $6000 annual retail cost of drugs
Retail cost of drug per month $500   Example of a 33% Co-Pay Tier Drug

Plan Phase	Month	Retail Cost of RX	You Pay	RX Plan Pays	Manufacturer Pays	Government Pays
Deductible Phase	January	$500	$360	$0	$0	$360
Initial Coverage	January		$47	$93	$0	$500
	February	$500	$165	$335	$0	$1,000
	March	$500	$165	$335	$0	$1,500
	April	$500	$165	$335	$0	$2,000
	May	$500	$165	$335	$0	$2,500
	June	$500	$165	$335	$0	$3,000
	July	$190	$63	$127	$0	$3,185
Coverage Gap	July	$310	$140	$16	$155	$3,310
	August	$500	$225	$25	$250	$3,798
	September	$500	$225	$25	$250	$4,285
	October	$479	$158	$321	$100	$4,850
Catastrophic	October	$21	$1	$20	$0	$4,871
	November	$500	$25	$475	$0	$5,371
	December	$500	$25	$475	$0	$5,871

	Retail	You Pay
Total	$ 6,000	$2,094

If you have selected a Medicare Advantage Plan, skip this summary

If you selected a Medigap plan and a prescription drug plan, read on

Summary

If you only take one generic medication you may find it beneficial to select the Part D plan that has a low premium and a high $360 deductible. Buy the Part D plan and don't use it. Just pay the low, $4 co-pay at any pharmacy and consider this your best option.

If you take several name-brand expensive prescriptions, you will definitely reap the benefits from selecting the most appropriate drug plan for your current drug needs. The prescription Part D plan you select could save you thousands of dollars over the course of the year. Go to Appendix F and follow the directions to use Medicare's website to select the most cost effective plan for your needs.

Refer to Appendix F for a guide on how to do this on Medicare's website at Medicare.gov. Keep the plan selection tool from Appendix G handy as you complete this process. The prescription drugs you are taking are what www.Medicare.gov relies on when matching you with the appropriate Medicare Part D Prescription Drug Plan.

IMPORTANT: A broker and/or insurance agent cannot ask you to provide any information about prescription drugs. By law, that is information you must provide on your own accord if they are to assist you with this process.

Chapter Five:
Enrollment Periods

"It is important to act timely; but, you also have to use an adequate amount of your time to choose the most appropriate option for your needs."

-David P. Schaeffer

When you become eligible to enroll in Medicare, it is important to act quickly; but, you also have to use an appropriate amount of your time to choose the very best option. Below is a basic breakdown of what to expect for enrollment periods. At the bottom of each page will be a visual in which each block represents a month beginning with when you are able to enroll, and ending with the conclusion of the open enrollment period where applicable. For each component, Easy Eddie will provide a bit more clarity about the enrollment period.

Part A

You have a guaranteed issue window of three months prior to, and three months after you turn 65 to purchase a Medigap Plan. You are guaranteed acceptance in this time period, without any medical questions asked.

Eligible to enroll

Birthday Month

Part B

Medicare Part B

You may choose to enroll in Part B anytime three months prior and three months after your 65th birthday month of eligibility. (Most folks enroll in Medicare Parts A and B at the same time)

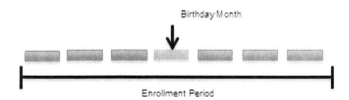

Birthday Month

Enrollment Period

Part D

Medicare Part D

You may select a Part D anytime three months prior and three months after your 65th birthday month of eligibility.

Note: There will be an ongoing future penalty if you do not enroll during this initial period of eligibility.

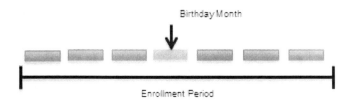

Medigap
(Medicare Supplement)

Medigap
(Medicare Supplement)

You have a guaranteed issue window of three months prior to, and three months after you turn 65 to purchase a Medigap Plan. You are guaranteed acceptance in this time period, without any medical questions asked.

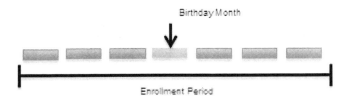

Birthday Month

Enrollment Period

Medicare Advantage

Medicare Advantage

You have a guaranteed issue window of three months prior to, and three months after you turn 65 to purchase a Medicare Advantage Plan. You are guaranteed acceptance in this time period, without any medical questions asked.

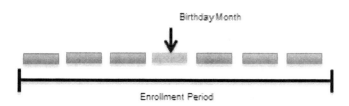

Birthday Month

Enrollment Period

Chapter Six:
Choosing an Insurance Agent or Broker

"Who will visit you in the hospital when you need assurance the most? Your local agent? Or, an outsourced telephone representative on the other side of the world?"

-David P. Schaeffer

Do I even need an agent?

Well, the simple answer is "Yes." You are going to have to deal with a licensed insurance agent at some point in the process, no matter what.

Whether you go to the company directly, or to an independent agent or broker, the premiums will be exactly the same!
My recommendation is to find someone you like and trust. It will make this entire process easier, and they can ensure that the choice you may have made on your own is truly the best option for your needs.

I have developed a few key questions to ask your agent or broker before you choose to do business with them to make sure that they truly have your best interest in mind.

Questions For Your Insurance Agent/Broker

1. Are they a local agent licensed by the state in which you reside? OR do they live in another state?

2. How many plans and carriers do they offer? We suggest offering at least 10 different insurance companies.

3. Do they have a bias toward one plan or another?

4. Do they have a dedicated live staff (real LOCAL people) to answer your questions when you need them the most? OR do they work out of the trunk of their car?

5. How many people have they helped select a Medicare plan and are those people willing to share their experiences with you?

6. Do they offer complete and comprehensive *side-by-side* comparison guides including EVERY plan in your area?

Our mission is simply to provide you with the tools and research you need to make the very best decision you can.

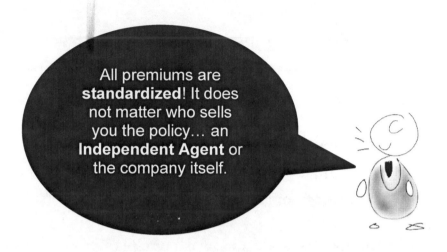

All premiums are **standardized**! It does not matter who sells you the policy… an **Independent Agent** or the company itself.

This is it. You made it! I hope that you have a more comfortable understanding of Medicare and are ready to experience 1-2-3 Easy!

Where can I go for more information?

For more information, feel free to visit www.Medicare.gov, www.123EasyMedicare.com, or www.AmericanRetire.com for

quick reference, or if you are in the Scottsdale, Arizona area, feel free to give us a call toll free at 877-220-1089, and schedule an appointment to come and chat, I would be happy to help.

Appendix A

COVERED COSTS of PART A

1.   Hospital Care

-Semi-private rooms, meals, general nursing and drugs.

-Care at acute care hospitals, critical access hospitals, in-patient rehabilitation facilities, long-term care hospitals.

IMPORTANT

Staying overnight in a hospital does NOT mean you are an in-patient. The doctor must formally admit you as such. MAKE SURE TO ALWAYS CHECK IF YOU ARE AN IN-PATIENT OR OUT-PATIENT with Part A (if you have a Medigap plan, it doesn't matter, it's COVERED).

2.   Skilled Nursing Facility Care

-3 day minimum medically necessary in-patient hospital stays, for a related illness or injury.

-You pay nothing for the first 20 days.

-You pay a coinsurance (percentage you pay of the cost, usually 20%) for days 21-100.

-After 100 days you pay ALL costs.

Appendix B

COVERED COSTS of PART B (you pay 20%)

The list below provides a basic list of the components of costs that Medicare will cover. Inside each one, there are multiple fees for services and treatments that are not covered. This is where the Medigap and Medicare Advantage plans come in to fill the gaps in coverage to ELIMINATE those hidden fees and charges that would otherwise be your responsibility.

1. Abdominal aortic aneurysm screening
2. Alcohol misuse screening and counseling
3. Ambulance services
4. Ambulatory surgical centers
5. Blood
6. Bone mass measurement (bone density)
7. Breast cancer screening (mammograms)
8. Cardiac rehabilitation
9. Cardiovascular disease (behavioral therapy)
10. Cardiovascular disease screenings
11. Cervical and vaginal cancer screening
12. Chemotherapy
13. Chiropractic services (limited coverage)
14. Clinical research studies
15. Colorectal cancer screenings

16. Defibrillator (implantable automatic)
17. Depression screening
18. Diabetes screenings
19. Diabetes self-management training
20. Diabetes supplies
21. Doctor and other health care provider services
22. Durable medical equipment (like wheelchairs)
23. EKG or ECG (electrocardiogram) screening
24. Emergency department services
25. Eyeglasses (limited)
26. Federally qualified health center services
27. Flu shots
28. Foot exams and treatment
29. Glaucoma tests
30. Hearing and balance exams
31. Hepatitis B shots
32. HIV screening
33. Home health services
34. Kidney dialysis services and supplies
35. Kidney disease education services
36. Laboratory services
37. Medical nutrition therapy services Mental health care (outpatient)
38. Obesity screening and counseling
39. Occupational therapy
40. Outpatient medical and surgical services and supplies

41. Physical therapy

42. Pneumococcal shot

43. Prescription drugs (limited)

44. Prostate cancer screenings

45. Prosthetic/orthotic items

46. Pulmonary rehabilitation

47. Rural health clinic services

48. Second surgical opinions

49. Sexually transmitted infections screening and counseling

50. Speech-language pathology services

51. Surgical dressing services

52. Telehealth

53. Tests (other than lab tests)

54. Tobacco-use cessation counseling

55. Transplants and immunosuppressive drugs

56. Urgently needed care

57. "Welcome to Medicare" preventive visit

58. Yearly "Wellness" visit

Appendix C

Surcharges to Monthly Premiums For Medicare Part B & D

(Income Related Monthly Adjustment Amounts)

The standard premium for Medicare Part B as of 2016 is $104.90 if you are already collecting Social Security. If you are not yet collecting Social Security this amount is $121.80

There are contingencies that apply. The following chart explains any additional costs.

Modified Adjusted Gross Income (MAGI)	Part B Monthly Cost	Part D Monthly Cost
-Individuals with a MAGI of $85,000 or less -Married Couples with a MAGI of $170,000 or less	Standard Premium Medicare Part B = **$104.90** (collecting Social Security) **$121.80** (If not collecting Social Security)	Your Medicare Part D Prescription Drug Plan Premium
-Individuals with a MAGI of $85,000 up to $107,000 -Married Couples with a MAGI of $170,000 up to $214,000	Part B Standard Premium + $48.70 = **$170.50**	Your Part D Plan Premium **+ $12.70**
-Individuals with a MAGI of $107,000 up to $160,000 -Married Couples with a MAGI above $214,000 up to $360,000	Part B Standard Premium + $121.80 = **$243.60**	Your Part D Plan Premium **+ $32.80**
-Individuals with a MAGI of $160,000 up to $214,000 -Married Couples with a MAGI above $360,000 up to $428,000	Part B Standard Premium + $194.90 = **$316.70**	Your Part D Plan Premium **+ $52.80**
-Individuals with a MAGI above $214,000 -Married Couples with a MAGI above $428,000	Part B Standard Premium + $268.00 = **$389.80**	Your Part D Plan Premium **+ $72.90**

Appendix D

CASE-by-CASE SELECTION CHART

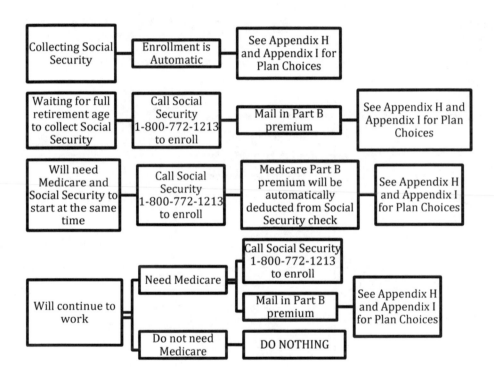

Appendix E

Medicare Parts A and B

Employer Group Health Plan				Medigap	Medicare Advantage	Medicaid

Call benefits department to see what is required			If cost is an issue	Part D	See Plan Selection Tool in Appendix G	Medicare Part B Premium waived

Part D included	Part D not included	If they say "Do Nothing", do nothing	See Chart in Appendix H for Medigap Plans A-N or Appendix I for Medicare Advantage Plans	See Appendix F for how to compare plans	Check Provider Directories	Qualifies for Social Security's Low Income Subsidy for Prescription Drugs (LIS)

	See Appendix F for how to compare plans		Weigh cost vs. coverage	Medigap Plans A-N	Check Perscription Drug List from Plan Selection Tool	

				See Chart in Appendix H	See Appendix F for guide to Medicare Perscription Drug Selection tool	

Appendix F

Choosing a Prescription Drug Plan

On www.Medicare.gov

Step 1

This is the home page of Medicare.gov. From here you need to hover your mouse over the "Drug Coverage" (Part D) tab. A drop down menu will appear; from this menu you need to click "Find health and drug plans" (Health Plans are the same thing as Medicare Advantage Plans).

Step 2

Type in your zip code in the highlighted box to find the plans available in your area.

Step 3

I am going to select the choices "I don't have any Medicare coverage yet" and "I don't get any extra help." This is just an example. If your case is different, feel free to select the options that are particular to your case. The following steps will be identical. This screen serves to narrow or expand the field of options available to you.

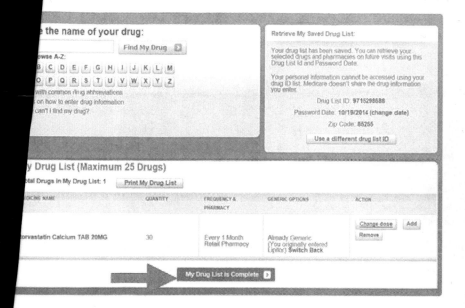

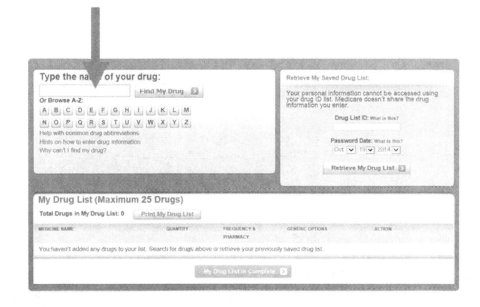

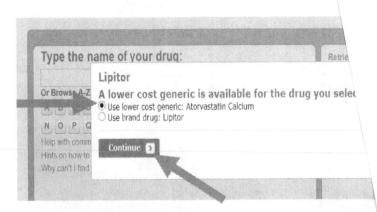

I am going to use Lipitor® as an example. I am simply going to click "Add drug and dosage" to continue.

The next screen will tell me if there are any generic medi available. I am going to choose to go with the generic nal drug, and click "Continue."

CPSIA information can be obtained at www.ICGtesting.com
Printed in the USA
LVOW11s2205130716

496174LV00004B/676/P

Step 4

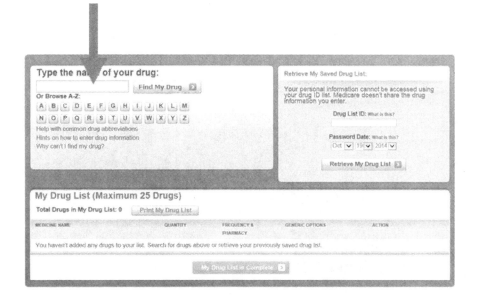

This is where the plan selection worksheet will come in handy. You can type in the box above up to 25 different prescription drugs that you are taking. The next screen brings up your options. It will show you exactly what you would be paying, with and even without the particular prescription drug plan.

Step 5

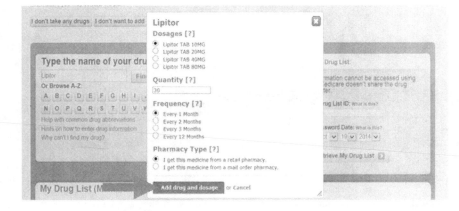

I am going to use Lipitor® as an example. I am simply going to click "Add drug and dosage" to continue.

Step 6

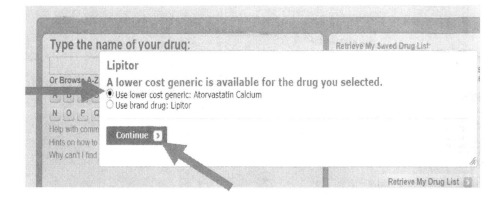

The next screen will tell me if there are any generic medications available. I am going to choose to go with the generic name drug, and click "Continue."

Step 7

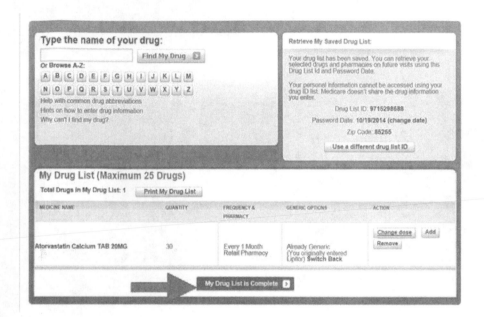

This next screen will then bring up the full list of drugs that I have entered. If you have more than one you would like to see about, just repeat steps 4-6 until you are finished. Once your list is complete, click "My drug list is complete."

Step 8

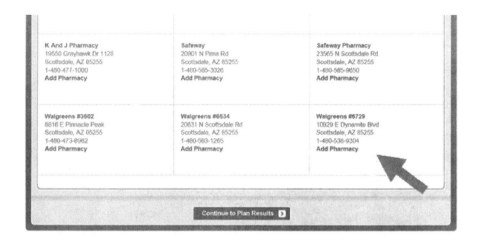

From here you need to choose your favorite or local pharmacy that you will use to pick up your medications. Some drug plans only work at particular pharmacies. Walgreens seems to be the most popular with the plans available. When you see the one you would like to select click "Add Pharmacy."

Step 9

Make sure that the pharmacy you wanted appears as the one
above. If the information is correct, then click "Continue to plan
results."

Mind that you can get a lower co-pay with a drug company's
plan when the drug store is a "preferred provider."

Step 10

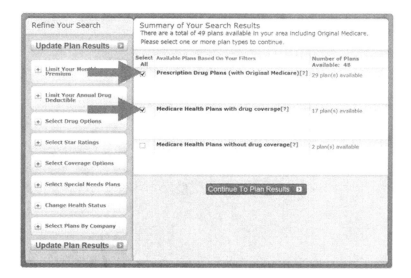

This screen presents you with another set of options. You can choose to only see Part D prescription drug plans, or you can see Medicare Advantage (Medical Health Plans), or all of the above at the same time. I am going to select the first two options, to see my options with Medicare Part D, and Medicare Advantage prescription plans.

Step 11

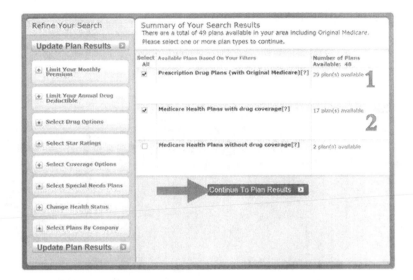

1.   Part D adds to your Medicare Supplement
2.   These are the Medicare Advantage plans

Once you make your selection click "Continue to plan results."

Step 12

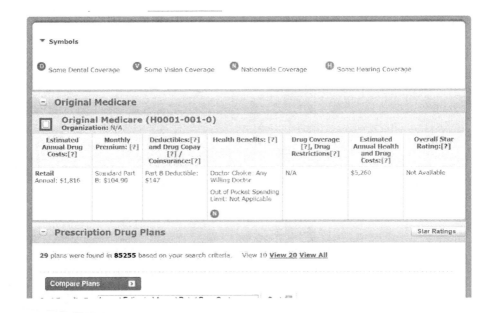

The first table will show you the cost of your prescriptions with just Medicare Parts A and B (Original Medicare).

Step 13

If we scroll down, we will begin to see our options with Part D prescription drug plans. We know this because of the PDP in the name of the plan.

Here you can see how much the plan will cost monthly, and annually. You can also see the deductibles and co-pays that are involved with each one of the plans

Make sure you look at the costs carefully, if you take a prescription. It may be worth paying a dollar or two more a month to eliminate a deductible or co-pay.

Step 14

If we keep scrolling down we will find the section titled "Medicare Health Plans with Drug Coverage" this is where we will find the Medicare Advantage drug coverage plans. The menus are the same, but you will notice in the names of the plans there is an (HMO) versus the (PDP) with the Part D plans.

You can select as many plans as you want from the menus by clicking the check box on the left. Once you have made your selections, click the big orange box that reads "Compare Plans."

Step 15

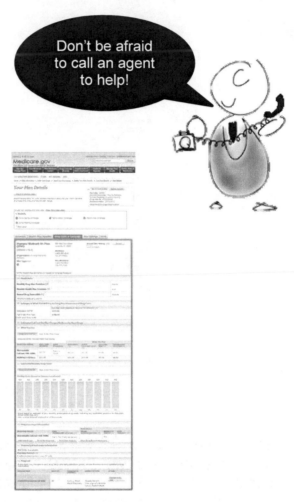

This screen will appear telling you more specifics of the plan you selected. The green tabs allow you to see a variety of different tables of information, from costs to customer reviews.

Feel free to repeat steps 8-14 to explore the possibilities when it comes to your prescription drug plan.

Appendix G

Medicare Advantage
Plan Selection Tool

Physicians	Specialty	Plan 1 Network	Plan 2 Network	Plan 3 Network	Plan 4 Network	Plan 5 Network	Plan 6 Network						
1 Physicians Name													
	PCP												
	PCP												
	Cardio												
	Chiro												
	other												
	other												
2 Hospitals													
	other												
3 Prescription Name	Dosage	/day											
4 Preferred Pharmacy:			Preferred Pharmacy:										
Alternate Pharmacy:			Alternate Pharmacy:										

Appendix H

New Medigap Plans (After June 1, 2010) – Medigap Plans A Through N

Medigap policies (including Medicare Select) can only be sold in eleven standardized plans. This chart gives you a quick look at all the Medigap plans and their benefits. Read down to find out what benefits are in each plan. If you need more information call your State Insurance Department.

A	B	C	D	F High Deductible	F	G	K	L	M	N
Basic Benefits, including 100% **Part B** co-insurance	Basic Benefits, including 100% **Part B** co-insurance	Basic Benefits, including 100% **Part B** co-insurance	Basic Benefits, including 100% **Part B** co-insurance	Benefits, including 100% Part B co-insurance After $2,180 deductible is reached	Basic Benefits, including 100% **Part B** co-insurance	Basic Benefits, including 100% **Part B** co-insurance	Basic Benefits, including 100% **Part B** co-insurance	Hospital and preventative care paid at 100%; other benefits paid at 50%	Hospital and preventative care paid at 100%; other benefits paid at 75%	Basic Benefits, including 100% Part B Co-insurance. Except up to $20 copayment for office visit, up to $50 copayment ER
		100% **Skilled Nursing** Coinsurance	100% **Skilled Nursing** Coinsurance	100% **Skilled Nursing** Coinsurance After $2,180 deductible is reached	100% **Skilled Nursing** Coinsurance	100% **Skilled Nursing** Coinsurance	50% **Skilled Nursing** Coinsurance	75% **Skilled Nursing** Coinsurance	100% **Skilled Nursing** Coinsurance	100% **Skilled Nursing** Coinsurance
	100% Medicare **Part A Deductible**	100% Medicare **Part A Deductible**	100% Medicare **Part A Deductible**	100% Medicare Part A Deductible After $2,180 deductible is reached	100% Medicare **Part A Deductible**	100% Medicare **Part A Deductible**	50% Medicare **Part A Deductible**	75% Medicare **Part A Deductible**	50% Medicare **Part A Deductible**	100% Medicare **Part A Deductible**
		100% Medicare **Part B Deductible**		100% Medicare Part B Deductible After $2,180 deductible is reached	100% Medicare **Part B Deductible**			100% Medicare **Part B Deductible**		
				100% Medicare Part B Excess Charges After $2,180 deductible is reached	100% Medicare **Part B Excess Charges**	100% Medicare **Part B Excess Charges**		100% Medicare **Part B Excess Charges**		
		80% Foreign Travel Emergency	80% Foreign Travel Emergency	80% Foreign Travel Emergency	80% Foreign Travel Emergency	80% Foreign Travel Emergency			80% Foreign Travel Emergency	80% Foreign Travel Emergency
							Out-of-pocket limit $4960; paid at 100% after limit reached	Out-of-pocket limit $2480; paid at 100% after limit reached		

Callout notes:

- This is the 20% GAP paid by your supplement.
- Medicare pays for 20 days, your supplement will pay until day 100.
- This year your Hospital deductible is $1,288 per visit, your supplement will pay this for you.
- This year your Doctor deductible is $166 per year, your supplement will pay this for you.
- If your doctor does not participate in Medicare, 100% of Doctor bill will be paid by your supplement.
- Medicare does not cover you outside the USA, your supplement will pay 80% after a $250 deductible.
- If your doctor charges above Medicare assigned amounts, your supplement will pay the excess charges up to 20%.

References

www.Medicare.gov

www.123EasyMedicare.com

www.AmericanRetire.com

About the Authors

Ian Schaeffer

Being born in Las Vegas, Nevada gave Ian an edge on understanding risk vs. reward at a very early age. It also showed him how to make sure goals are successfully achieved by playing the odds to his advantage.

As a young man studying Industrial Engineering at Northeastern University, Mr. Schaeffer knows a thing or two about wrapping his arms around large, multi-faceted projects and breaking them down into process-driven, manageable tasks. His experience ranges from designing six-sigma process control systems on the manufacturing floor to implementing lean principles improving data flow and effective cross function and departmental communication in the insurance and wealth management space.

Like his father, Ian likes to write, speak in public, and most of all, help others accomplish their goals.

David Schaeffer

For over 16 years, David Schaeffer has been advising folks just like you on how to navigate the mysteries of Medicare. Thousands of retiree's, including past employees of AAA, American Airlines, Banner Healthcare, Boeing, Caremark, Honeywell, IBM, Intel, Pitney Bowes, and the State of Arizona have gone to Mr. Schaeffer for his expertise in transitioning from group and individual health plans to Medicare.

You may recognize Mr. Schaeffer from his articles on the changes in Medicare in "The American Retirement Advisor". Additionally he has founded several online self-service web sites to provide research previously not available to the general public, such as 123EasyMedicare.com, providing side-by-side comparisons of every choice facing a person new to Medicare. Mr. Schaeffer is also one of only 7,000 retirement planners to have been awarded the Certified Senior Advisor (CSA) designation in the United States. Mr. Schaeffer lives in Cave Creek with his wife, Thea, and their two children. When he's not busy educating retirees on ways to preserve their quality of life, he likes to work on his sailing skills.

David and Ian Schaeffer